to Fred Roden,

It was a pleasure to see you
and Joe when you visited
La Baraka - Thank you for
being such a wonderful friend
to Bob. We hope to see you
again soon - Have a very
Happy birthday!

Best wishes

8/30/18   Annette

Jean-Luc and Lucette

Behind That Smile

A Memoir

∽

by

Lucette Sonigo

My brother, Guy

Dedication

To Guy, my brother, my hero, my guardian angel, who spread his wings to protect me, who shared with me all his strength, all his knowledge, and all his wisdom so that I could stand up against all odds.

Thank you, Guy!

To You, To Life!

L'Chaim!

Table of Contents

Our friends from the Oratorio Society
David and Lee Ann Close

Our dear friends Bob and Linda Martin

Acknowledgments

With thanks and blessings to all our friends!

Thirty-eight years after the opening of La Baraka, we want to thank Nelly, Pierre, Jacky, and Raoul for sponsoring us to come to the United States. Maria and Tony Sorace gave us the hospitality of their home. Lilian and Bernie Zwerling opened our eyes with precious advice. Nick and Agnes, from the Village Coffee Shop in Great Neck, opened their arms and their kitchen to our whole family. Thank you to Emile and Jeanne Tubiana. Without their help, La Baraka would have never been born. Tamara and Igor Vassiliev put the deed to their property on the line so we could get more financial help from the bank. Thanks to David and Lee Ann Close for filling up the restaurant with their friends from the "Oratorio Society"; Mr. and Mrs. Spar for all those years of fidelity and making sure that the next generation keeps us as busy as they did; Mr. Douglas, who attended all of our special celebrations and brought along all of his friends; Mark and Terri, who joined us for so many special occasions; and Linda and Bob Martin, who celebrate our anniversaries and birthdays with us and provide wonderful presents. Thank you to our next-door neighbors, Peter and Carmen from the Beauty Shop, who encouraged their patrons to try our food; to Elaine Greenbaum, a former opera singer, who calls La Baraka her second home; and to Mr. and Mrs. Lehr, boating enthusiasts who said of our restaurant, "It's a port in the storm."

Thank you to Viviane Tubiana for all of her support and for designing such a beautiful cover.

Thanks to Michael Chatham for his design expertise, and to Stacy Cortigiano for her production and copy-editing skills.

Special thanks to my friend and editor Bob Tilton for his help, for the confidence he had in me and my stories, and for his tenacity, pushing me and providing positive energy when I was discouraged. And thank you to his wife, Rita, for her friendship and patience.

To our daughter Valerie, who worked by our sides when her busy schedule permitted it, I offer my heartfelt gratitude, appreciation, and love.

Introduction

What's behind that smile?

It is a long story, a long life filled with interesting events and circumstances, some happy, some sad, all hidden by a smile.

Dear reader, please do not think that I am looking for any pity or bemoaning my fate. My goal is to show you, particularly my children and my friends, how an optimistic frame of mind can help to overcome any situation and apply at least a temporary balm to a broken heart.

Many of the events described in the opening section of this memoir, "An Orphan's Journey," were related to me by my brother, my grandmother, her friends, and her neighbors who had survived the atrocities of World War II. I remember my school years quite clearly. It is sometimes said of senior citizens that they remember events from fifty years ago more precisely than what happened fifty minutes ago. This is perhaps true, but in looking back now, I see how the challenges that I faced as a child molded me into the woman I became. To know me well, one should have a sense of the whole story. The second section, "La Baraka," concerns the opening of the restaurant, while the third section, "Pressure Cooker," is made up of a number of anecdotes from our time in

Little Neck. My hope is that you get a sense of where what people have called my "gift" for being unflappable came from.

I

An Orphan's Journey

Lucette's parents, Adèle and Victor Fitoussi

My Family

My life started on the 24th of April, 1941. I was born in a little town called Béja in the north of Tunisia in North Africa. Many farms surrounded the village. The wheat would grow very high in the fields; our region was known as "the breadbasket of Tunisia." Many mills ground the wheat into semolina and other types of flour. Every spring the storks arrived and rested on our roofs, clapping their beaks and flapping their wings as they searched for branches with which to build their nests. (It is one of the few places, among them the Alsace region of France, where they would settle down until autumn.) The symbol of Béja was the stork; a huge one stood at the entrance to the town. My grandmother told me that one of them brought me to my parents! Since the departure of those farmers after Tunisia's independence, the wheat fields have become rows of sugar beets. A giant sugar refinery with its tall chimneys has changed the landscape. Béja is now called "the sugar of Tunisia."

In the spring of 1941, my family welcomed a chubby girl, who followed her eight-year-old sister, Simone,

**Lucette's grandmother
Leila Fitoussi**

and five-year-old brother, Guy. My father was a furniture builder; my mother, Adèle, stayed at home to raise us. My ancestors on my father's side came from Spain. They had escaped the deadly Inquisition and the pogrom against the Jewish community in 1490. My mother's family came from Livorno, Italy; they were also persecuted for their beliefs. My grandmother Leila was the pillar of our family, not only because of her age, but because of her strong character and experience. She would play a very important role in the lives of my brother and myself. Leila never went to a French school, and she spoke only Arabic, which I learned at an early age. She lived in a large, beautiful house that had been built by the Spanish ancestors. They were Sephardic and they were very religious people. They built a synagogue on the second floor of their house above the bedrooms. The walls were covered with mosaic tiles; the windows were protected by wrought iron. It looked like the Alhambra.

A large court surrounded by columns contained several rooms. Polygamy was permitted in Tunisia, but my male ancestors did not have numerous wives. (In some homes, the man of the house would settle a wife in each bedroom!)

My parents had an apartment in town on the third floor of a beautiful white building surrounded by flowers and bushes. The apartment had a long balcony that faced City Hall. Simone and Guy attended the elementary school. Mom or Dad would pick them up at the end of the day. We all lived happily, but it would not be so "ever after."

Lucette at nine months (fifteen days before the catastrophe)

The War

When I was born, Tunisia was a battleground. World War II raged around us. The Germans had invaded the country from many directions: Algeria in the west, Libya in the south, and Sicily in the north. The French army and their American allies had settled around Béja, spreading their brown tents like a web to hide their trucks and other equipment from the enemy. In the town, long lines of people waited for food and other supplies. Everyone was worried about the situation. No one knew what would happen from one day to the next. Sirens would warn the inhabitants to search for shelter in the event of an attack.

The German troops were rapidly approaching, their trucks and tanks crawling like long snakes along the roads. Their hope was to surprise the French and American armies. When they arrived about twenty-five kilometers from Béja, at the door of an Allied encampment, a deadly battle ensued that shook the countryside. The troops led by Generals Rommel and Patton fought to the last drop of blood. Over three thousand French and American soldiers were killed. (Today you can visit the well-kept cemetery where many of them were buried.) The population of the town was terrified. Families tried to group together to share the available shelters.

According to our next-door neighbors, on Friday, November 20, 1942, my mother was at home cooking, preparing for the Shabbat. One of them, Madame Taieb, remembered that our house always smelled wonderful, a testament to Mom's good cooking. Especially on Shabbat, all of the spices from the succulent salads, for the *apéritif* and the steaming couscous, fragrant with cumin, coriander, and mint, permeated the atmosphere. Simone was helping by setting the table, covering it with a beautiful lace tablecloth and shiny silverware. She was happy; although she was only eight, Simone had taken on some of the responsibilities of a young lady. As she worked, she was rehearsing all of the songs that she had learned in school. I was asleep in my crib. My parents had decided that once everyone was at home, they would not leave our apartment; they hoped that our family would be spared.

My father and Guy were on their way back after visiting my grandmother. My mother was anxiously awaiting their arrival, showing her impatience by looking from the balcony every five minutes. Suddenly a loud siren was heard, a warning that an attack was imminent. The sky above our building became black with roaring German bombers. The sound was like thunder. My mother screamed, picked me up from my crib, and ran to get my sister to take her downstairs. She was too late. A dozen bombs were dropped, aimed at the Béja City Hall. Some of them landed on our roof. The three-story building trembled and fell like a house of cards. Heavy smoke and dust filled the area. Chaotic sounds — screams, cries, more sirens — filled the air.

Everyone from the neighborhood came running to the rescue. There was panic near the demolished area. My father was not too far away, still walking toward the apartment. When he saw the smoke, he started to run, forcing Guy to follow as fast as his little legs could carry him. When they arrived at the scene, my father began crying, holding his head, and screaming the names of my mother and sister. Ambulances and fire engines soon surrounded the site, the firemen pushing back the curious and helping the volunteers who had begun to search for survivors. Some human shapes were pulled from the debris; many were not able to stand up. They were covered with blood, ashes, and dust, but they were alive. One digger yelled, "I hear a baby crying on this side!" My father and some other men ran to the spot. They had to remove stones, wood, glass, and ashes. Eventually they pulled me out, black from the soot and screaming my lungs out. Other than a few cuts and bruises, I was generally healthy. My father squeezed me in his arms, sobbing and thanking God. A nurse took me away with Guy, who was also sobbing. He was only six years old, but he remembered every detail of that day, which he told me about when I was old enough to understand.

The crew continued their digging. A few hours later, they had pulled out ten bodies, not a breath of life in any of them. It was very distressful and emotional when they recognized who had been killed. Two of the bodies belonged to my mother and my sister. They were found hugging, as if they were tied together. My father fell on his knees, crying. There was nothing that could have been done to save them. It was a tragedy for our family and for so many other innocent families caught in the middle of a war.

My grandmother, who heard about the bombing in the town, came to the site and took Guy and me to her own house. Her single daughter, tata Marcelle, and her bachelor son, tonton David, gave us a bath and some food, and put us to bed. After the funeral, the house was filled with friends offering condolences and many types of food. I was carried from arms to arms, always followed by Guy, who didn't let me out of his sight. Grandma and tata Marcelle pampered me like a nine-month-old baby should be pampered.

In truth, the family was devastated. My father and uncle each grew a beard, according to Jewish tradition. Guy was skinny, with a sad and serious face for his age, while I grew chubbier and happier. Very often Guy took me in his arms; eventually he played an important role in teaching me how to walk, perhaps so that he would have someone to play soccer with. My father, who had been called by the French Armed Forces prior to the bombing, returned to work to finish pieces of furniture that he had promised to deliver.

A few weeks later, the Germans returned to retrieve what was left of their army and their equipment. The area was devastated. After they had left, other German soldiers came. They were prisoners who were forced to clean up the town under heavy French guard. Many buildings were completely or partially destroyed. The people were mourning the deaths of loved ones; neighbors tried to comfort neighbors, but there was little consolation to be found. There were no religious barriers in Tunisia; this was especially true in Béja. The population was a mix of Muslims, Jews, and Christians, many of the latter being descendants of Sicilian families. Everyone had to pick up the pieces and rebuild what was destroyed by human greed and hatred. Napoleon's defeat had not been a powerful enough lesson after all.

My father came home each night extremely tired. He was eating very little, but he always gave us his attention and his love. One morning, after shaving and getting ready to go to work, he fainted. He was running a very high temperature. My grandmother forced him to stay in bed and called the doctor. The diagnosis fell like another bomb on our house — typhus. He had caught the deadly disease while on military duty. As the days went by, Dad struggled between moments of delirium, when he would call out for his wife and daughter, and moments of lucidity.

One night my grandmother woke up Guy. My father was having a bad night and wanted to talk to his son. Guy sat by Dad's bedside and held his hands. He promised, from that moment on, to be the "man of the house" and to always take care of me. My father died that same night, like a candle blown out by a breeze. We had lost the two people who were supposed to be the pillars of our future.

I was too young to realize the dangerous situation we were in, but poor Guy! He had a broken heart, he was suddenly responsible for himself and his baby sister, and he was only six years old. From that day on, he took me under his wing; he kept his promise to our father. There was never a time since when I did not feel Guy's benevolent presence, even when we were hundreds or thousands of miles apart.

The war finally ended. The Germans had been defeated. But this did not stop the chaos in many of the formerly occupied countries. We were staying at our grandmother's house. The French government appointed a guardian for Guy and me. It was tonton David, my father's brother, who was single and bitter. We were each granted a decent pension until the age of twenty-one, a free scholarship, and many other social advantages. We had new stamps added to our birth certificates: *pupille de la nation*, which meant "orphans because of the war." We were thereby adopted by the French nation. This did not replace the precious family that we had lost. After our father's death, our crusade for life started. Guy knew that our childhood would be short. He had to think and act like an adult.

Lucette and Guy, 1946

After the War

Guy gained a few pounds during this period, while I got chubbier and chubbier. Soon I was ready to begin walking in earnest. Tata Marcelle baked the bread and covered the slices with the hot sauce called *harissa* and olive oil. It was Guy's *filet mignon*. She created a doll out of old socks, and she sewed some dresses for me, which I also tried on the cat, Minouche, ending up with scratches on my hands and many tears.

Guy wanted to stay in good shape. He was a fervent admirer of the boxer Marcel Cerdan, whom Édith Piaf loved so much. Guy tried to practice on me. His hits came down like heavy rain; sometimes he forgot who he was and who I was, a toddler barely standing on my feet. A head-butt knocked me down and out. Horrified and scared, he slapped my face until I woke up and cried. The result was that he was put in the corner for an hour.

My Second Chance

Tata Marcelle took care of Guy and me as my mother would have done. She pampered me and put me to sleep with beautiful lullabies. One morning she came to my crib to change my diaper. She lifted me in her arms. As she looked down to retrieve the sock I had lost, she screamed, "Oh my God!" Right there, where I had been in the crib, was a huge, black scorpion, apparently sound asleep. I guess my peepee worked like an anesthetic. Tonton David and Guy came running to take the scorpion away. Because it was a very old house, my grandmother said that she had seen a few of them, but none of that size.

That was my second chance to live, to stay in this world and make the best of it. In retrospect, it seems, like a cat, I had many more lives to live.

First Separation

The schools were closed for several months. When they reopened, Guy was finishing the last part of elementary school. He came to Grandma's each day for lunch. We all had dinner together. Our guardian soon registered him for a boarding school that was one hundred and twenty kilometers away. I still did not quite understand why Grandma and tata Marcelle were crying while they prepared his suitcase, but I began to cry too. In the morning they said goodbye. He was holding his luggage, tied up with a string; a beret covered his shaved head, and he wore a suit too big for him. When he walked away, Grandma threw a bucket of water behind him, a traditional gesture for a safe return, which wet his pants from the waist down. I did not understand that I wouldn't see him again for a while.

Kindergarten

At the age of three, my guardian took me to the preschool. The teacher, Madame Fratacci, happened to have had my mother in her class. She took me on her lap to console me, as I was scared and crying. She soon discovered a big handicap, as I naturally held the pen or the chalk in my left hand. She tied a little red ribbon to my right wrist to remind me to use that hand. Since then, when I have had a choice, such as when using scissors or a knife, I have used my left hand. I was a rare case, a curiosity. I hated to go to school, and I begged tata Marcelle not to send me there. But no matter where I had pains — my head, my stomach, anywhere else — I could not convince her to allow me to stay at home.

Behind That Smile

First Christmas

The Christmas holidays brought an end to my boredom without Guy. He was back! What a joy! He had lost his beret, which made our guardian furious. I jumped up to greet him, kissing his head and his hands. His face, however, was very serious; he seemed so sad. He began to teach me how to count on my fingers. I wished I was an octopus because none of my answers were right. Sometimes I had too many fingers and sometimes not enough. Guy was patient; he wanted me to be as smart as he was. His report card was excellent.

Guy and I were healthy and happy to be together. We played with marbles and apricot pits. Grandma prepared the stew that we loved and the traditional couscous on Friday nights. I always loved to sing and dance. Guy loved to read. He would tell me stories, exaggerating the scary parts so that he could enjoy my curiosity and laugh at my fears. Guy wanted me to be as strong as a *citadelle*.

He was my hero.

He is still my hero.

At one time, a neighbor offered to take us to the movie — there was only one movie theater in the town — to see *Tarzan* with Johnny Weissmuller. We were laughing at Cheetah the chimpanzee, and were amazed by the agility of the actors, especially Tarzan and Jane, who was so beautiful. I squeezed Guy's hand when I was afraid. What a wonderful time! Our first movie — we came out so happy. Our guardian was outside, waiting for us, in a very bad mood as usual. He could not dampen our spirits, however.

When we got home, Guy remembered that we had a very old wheelbarrow. He took it out to a very steep street around the corner from our house. We flew down the hill, feeling like wings were growing from our backs. We had to be equal to, or even better than, Tarzan! Guy ordered me to jump off the cart when it was at full speed! I jumped at his signal. What a bad idea! I fell flat on my stomach and was not able to breathe for a few seconds. My knees and my nose were bleeding. I would not cry! I had to show Guy how strong I was. We came home quietly. Thank God our guardian did not see us. Tata Marcelle cleaned me up, all the while scolding Guy for his lack of responsibility.

∾

Elementary School

When I reached the age of six, I was sent to the same boarding school that Guy attended. I was not sad because I knew that he was there. Grandma threw the traditional bucket of water, missing my new blue coat by an inch. What a warm feeling of security to know that my brother was at my side or, at the least, not too far away. I soon learned that he was not as close as I had hoped. The superintendents kept me away so that he could play soccer with his classmates after school hours without me bothering him. I had to stay in a corner with my hands above my head, not able to wipe away my tears. Guy was sad and sorry; he constantly turned his attention from the game. As soon as he could, he came to give me a hug and he called together some young girls to organize a game with me, in part to make me feel more at home and in part so that he could get back to his activities.

Because of the poor diet we were served and the generally poor hygiene at the school, my skin broke out. There were rough, red spots on my face. The nurse suspected that it might be contagious, so I could not share my towels with my friends. One week I was disinfected with a red liquid; another week I was treated with iodine, which was a yellow color. I still had to attend my classes, but now I always arrived back at my room a half hour late. Every time I opened the door, a general, loud laugh welcomed me. I was red faced or yellow faced. To push back my tears, I learned how to clown around instead. Other times, when I had an accident in bed, I had to wear the wet sheet on my head and go from classroom to classroom like a little ghost, trying to wipe away the mockeries in my heart.

The French government financed that orphanage. It was run by Catholic nuns. There was much to do, so an abundance of food and good hygiene were not their top priorities. Strict discipline was. The property was immense. It was the former palace of the Bey, who was the king of Tunisia before its independence. Marble and mosaics covered every room, and colorful gardens surrounded a huge monument. We had the king's slave quarters, which were plain and cold, for our dormitories. (Yes – it does get cold in North Africa!)

The classrooms were prefabricated and were also very cold. The teacher made us jump up and down to warm up our cold feet and bodies. It was fun, and that put us in a good mood and gave us lots of energy. I made a few friends, but I was always supervised by Guy when he was not in his own classroom. He was a very good student; I soon learned that he would graduate at the end of the year and go on to attend the senior high school, which was one hour away by train. All I could think was, "How am I going to survive in this orphanage without him?"

࿈

Behind That Smile

First Summer Vacation

At the end of June, Guy and I went back to Grandma's house for a week. As orphans adopted by the French government, we were entitled to two months of summer camp in France. Tata Marcelle prepared our very old suitcases, tied with strings, and our uncle bought us two new berets. We really looked like *poulbots* (street urchins) when we were dressed to go, but we were happy to share that wonderful trip. Grandma splashed us with a bucket of water for a safe return. We took the bus to the capital, Tunis, with our guardian; it was about one hundred and twenty kilometers from Béja. All of the children were reunited on the busy *place du marché* where buses were waiting to take us to the harbor.

A huge *paquebot*, all white with large chimneys and strident sirens, was calling to us and to hundreds of other passengers. We embarked with all of those children, who had come from so many different directions. After a cold goodbye from our uncle, we jumped on to the footbridge. We were also jumping for joy to be together and to leave behind our always-angry guardian.

The blue Mediterranean Sea was breathtaking! Some porpoises were following the boat, jumping right under our eyes as if to amuse us. After twenty-four hours of traveling, the French coast at Marseille appeared. The Château d'If was getting closer. Guy told me some of the stories from *Le Comte de Monte-Cristo*. When we reached the port, we all lined up and were counted like sheep. Buses were waiting to take us to the station. Then it would be eight hours more by train before we arrived at our destination. The region was in the Loire Valley; it was wooded and green, like nothing I had ever seen. The kings of France had built multitudes of sumptuous castles in this area over the centuries — to this day, everyone who goes to France must visit Les Châteaux de la Loire.

Our bus stopped in front of a small castle that had been donated by the town to serve as the headquarters for the orphans' vacation. It was called Selles-sur-Cher; it was very well known for goat cheese that was covered with ashes. The counselors provided plenty of activities for us: songs, dances, plays, and games. We also had plenty of fresh air and nutritional food. Guy gained a few pounds, and, of course, I got even chubbier. We were having a good time, seeing each other every day.

Two months went by very quickly. Soon it was time to pack our belongings and say goodbye to our new friends, promising to keep in touch with them. The trip back to Tunisia was long, but we had so many good memories of our time in France. After being dragged from the boat, to the train, to the bus, we arrived back in Tunis. Our guardian was waiting for us, along with the parents of some of the other children. He gave us each a cold hug while scolding us for not sending a postcard. He then asked us where our berets were!

After a bumpy bus trip, we arrived in Béja. Grandma and tata Marcelle were so happy to greet us and to see that our faces had become a little rounder. We had another week of vacation before we had to go back to school. Guy would be going to the *lycée* for boys, while I would be heading to the orphanage at L'Ariana, which was located in a suburb of Tunis.

I forgot to mention that my uncle had put in my suitcase some of Guy's clothes that had become too small for him. I inherited his pajamas, with a fly, and shoes that were five sizes too big, which always arrived before me when I was running.

Back to School

When I arrived at the boarding school along with my uncle, many of my friends were waiting at the gate. My new teacher was young and beautiful. Her name was Mademoiselle Clanet. She played an important role during the academic year that was to follow.

First, she made me promise to be as good a student as my brother. To me this was impossible! Guy was brilliant in every subject, he was serious when doing his homework, and he wrote poetry in his spare time! I said, "I'll try." She put her trust in me. I could not disappoint her. Guy tried to come and visit every weekend; he had to hitchhike, as he did not have enough money for the tramway. He kept most of his desserts during the week so that he would not come to me empty-handed. He was so happy to see me, to hug me. He was getting taller and more handsome.

Sitting with him, under the blossoms of the almond tree, we shared the goodies. Knowing my sweet tooth, he always gave me the bigger portion.

Oh my hero!

We would laugh together and he would read to me the most recent poems he had written. His own grades were very good, and he was proud of mine. He wanted me to be the smartest and strongest girl in my class. Guy reminded me that we had nobody to lean on or complain to but each other. The two hours that he would spend with me went by so fast. He had to return to his school in the same way he had come to visit — hitchhiking. It was always with a heavy heart that we parted.

My friends would sometimes wait for his departure to organize a game. I would accept, if only to keep from showing any tears. One day, while we were playing hide-and-seek, the elastic on my underwear gave up and there went my panties to my knees. We had a good laugh, but I did not know what to do. Two of my friends gave me their shoelaces, but then they could not run anymore. Another one gave me a hairpin. I fixed my panties as well as I could. That incident taught me from a very young age to find a solution to a problem before moaning or crying about it.

Back in class, I often found myself dreaming, looking out of the window, instead of studying. The trees were in bloom and the birds were nesting. It was interesting to observe them going back and forth with twigs and worms. I was so busy observing Mother Nature that I did not realize that Mademoiselle Clanet had twice called my name. She scolded me and reminded me to keep my attention in the classroom.

After classes we went to the large dining room, called the *réfectoire*, to do our homework. I did mine seriously and my teacher was very proud of my work. Very discreetly she would place some candies or chocolates in my schoolbag. I learned a lot during those years: the value of friendship and the importance of sharing whatever I had with my schoolmates (and they with me), be it pens, candies, chewing gum, or underwear. There were no denunciations between us. Very often we were deprived of desserts and put against the wall with our hands up for an hour because "Nobody did it." I learned compassion, dignity, patience, and how to defend myself against bullies. Even at this young age, ingenuity was my motto.

I soon noticed that my teacher was apparently flirting with another instructor named Monsieur Louman. I was a little jealous, but I was happy for her. She still gave me her attention, and I felt loved. She always encouraged me to do better in school and, perhaps more importantly, to be a better person. Mademoiselle Clanet and Monsieur Louman would take long walks in the alleys, between the bushes covered with colorful and aromatic flowers. The birds were probably singing to the rhythm of their hearts. I wished that I was their child! Was it a premonition?

Behind That Smile

Heartbreak

Two weeks before the end of June, I was called to the supervisor's office. I trembled, wondering what had gone wrong. My grades were good, I had no trouble with anyone — what could be the problem? I was shocked to see my guardian standing in the office, stiff as a dry stick. His eyes were on fire. I was ordered to pack my clothes and to leave the school immediately, without saying goodbye to anyone — not to my friends, not to my teacher.

The trip to my grandmother's house was torture. Not one word was exchanged. I still did not know what was happening. I later learned that Mademoiselle Clanet and her husband-to-be had written a letter to my uncle asking that they be allowed to adopt me. They promised to take very good care of my education. I did not know that they had done this! *Dommage!* How wonderful they both were! What a generous decision they had made!

I was heartbroken. I loved them both and did not want to leave them. The philosopher Voltaire once wrote "Tears are silent grief." I cried often when I thought of their kindness. Did my guardian show me any affection?

Was he simply afraid to lose the sizable pension paid by the French government? I never found out because he never showed me either one of them. As I thought about it, I considered that better days were ahead.

> *There is a flame in you called hope.*
> *As long as it keeps burning,*
> *it maintains your spiritual life.*

My Adolescence

With a very heavy heart, I began junior high school in my hometown. My guardian insisted that I live in a boarding school that was a few blocks away from my grandmother's house. My new schoolmates became my best friends very quickly. Therese, Marie-Antonia, Pendino, Morganti — all are very successful today and still write or call me after fifty-two years. I tried to be as good a student as they were so as not to be left behind. We organized some shows for the other students, some fun nights, helped by our best teacher, Mr. Goulard, who passed away in 2016 at the age of one hundred. They gave me private lessons to improve my mathematics, which was my weakest subject.

The end of the year approached rapidly. We had to pass a test called *brevet d'études* to go to college, as high school was called. Guy was already graduating. He, too, had to pass a difficult exam called *le baccalauréat*. We both had good results and were happy to celebrate at Grandma's when school was finished.

Guy had a surprise for me. He had applied for counselor positions for both of us in France. The organization would pay for the whole trip in addition to a small salary to take care of children during a two-month period during the summer. I jumped in his arms, screaming with happiness, thrilled to be spending part of the summer by his side. We stayed a week with Grandma. I learned how to sew with her help, using my left hand.

I made two pairs of shorts for the camp. We gathered decent clothes to put in better suitcases — no strings, no berets! I was a young lady by now, who had lost some of her chubbiness, and Guy was tall and handsome. We would have no more *poulbot* looks from others. The day of our departure soon arrived. After the goodbyes, and the half bucket of water thrown by our grandmother, we left town, by bus, for Tunis. A taxi took us to the harbor. We embarked on a huge boat called *Le Chanzy*. We met the captain and a few young men of the crew. Guy kept me by his side the whole time, protecting me from their glances and their questions. I must admit that I was proud to be noticed. After forty-eight hours of sailing, we saw Marseille. A hotel was provided where we would spend the night.

What a beautiful city! It was so colorful, with many busy streets. Many large avenues were bordered by elegant stores, trees, and flowers. The next morning, we took the train to Paris. We could not believe it. We were in the most romantic city in the world! It was precious for its historical past, its large monuments. Every place we saw, every bridge over the Seine, had a fascinating story. We saw Notre-Dame, Montmartre, la Concorde. We sometimes took the metro, but most of the time we walked, discovering district after district. We were impressed by the Eiffel Tower, although we could not go up to the top because the fare was too expensive. We mingled with the crowd at night — all those illuminations, the busy *cafés*, the musicians in the streets filled our hearts with joy and happiness. The next day we were meeting the people and the children from the camp.

I had eight children, each six years old, under my supervision. We settled in a concrete building. Guy had twelve youngsters between twelve and fourteen years old. They were sleeping under a tent. We had to keep all of them busy, so we provided a lot of activities. The town where the camp was, Les Mathes, was just a few kilometers from the ocean. When the weather permitted, we walked to the shore with the little ones, singing all the way. The specialties of the region were oysters and clams, which we searched for on the beach. I saw Guy every day. I would describe to him all of the details of my work day.

Two months went by very quickly. With tearful good-byes to our kids and to the other counselors, we packed our belongings and returned home the same way we had come, from train, to boat, to bus. We finally arrived in front of our door at eight o'clock at night. It was dark; we were tired, and we had little money left in our pockets, but we were happy. We knocked at the door. Nobody answered. Instead of the lock, there was a large hole, big enough to see inside. The place was empty, completely empty! Where were they? Where had they gone? The neighbor across the street came running over with her son. "They moved to Algiers! We thought that you knew!"

We did not know what to do. We both had tears in our eyes. We were speechless! The lady and her son, Victor, offered us hospitality for the night.

We were heartbroken! We hadn't seen our grandma and we didn't know when we would see her again. How about our personal items: our clothes, Guy's poems — he had written over one hundred of them — could we retrieve them? Even tired, we could not sleep. Victor told us that the French Embassy, which was located in Tunis, was looking for young people with the *baccalauréat* to teach Arabic students. The next morning we took the bus to Tunis.

Guy was hired right away. Our destination was La Goulette, a little harbor on the beach, only fifteen kilometers from the capital. The town was very popular for its avenue bordered by fish restaurants that served the summer vacationers. Claudia Cardinale, the famous Tunisian-born actress, would spend all of her summers there before moving to Hollywood.

We took a little white train to visit the school. We remembered that an old aunt had settled there many years ago. Everybody knew her because she read tarot cards. She was so happy to see us! She hugged us and started to cry because "I looked just like my mother." We slept at her home that night. The next day she found a furnished two-bedroom apartment for us with a kitchen. She vouched for us until Guy's first salary check arrived. How generous of her!

∞

Our Independence

We spent a week getting acquainted with the neighborhood and the neighbors, among whom was a lovely Italian couple, Madame Marie and Monsieur Joseph, with two children. Guy registered me for the *lycée*, which started at the beginning of October. I took the little train twice a day. I was so happy to be free and living with Guy. Every night was like a vacation night. We took long walks along the beach, cooking fast meals and enjoying our freedom.

He soon started teaching. His students were ten years old, all from Arabic families. They were learning French. Many times when Guy was grading the essays, he would burst into laughter because the literal translations from Arabic were often awkward. One student wrote: "My mother is in bed with the doctor!" which meant in Arabic, "She is so sick that we called the doctor!" In another paper, a student wrote: "My brother is playing the frog." In Arabic, *frog* means "mandolin."

During this time, I worked hard at my studies, and I was getting good reports at school.

The neighbors who gave us hospitality when my uncle left us in the street managed to find our address. I received a few letters from Victor. I responded, with Guy's permission, of course. Victor visited us many times. He took us to the movies and to restaurants. Guy was very protective and was always at my side. He did not want anyone to hurt me. I was attracted to Victor and touched by his mother's affection. At every reunion, I was spoiled with gifts and flowers.

Toward the end of June, after Victor had come to visit many times, he asked Guy if he could marry me! With tears in his eyes, my brother accepted. He was happy for me but sad and worried. I was only eighteen years old. In the meantime, the French Embassy had offered him a job in Paris. Although Guy was a teacher, he had entered a competition that was connected to French national television. Guy accepted a position as a producer and left Tunisia at the end of the summer. Before he left, he made a thousand recommendations to Victor about his sister's future. (Guy soon rose to the position of Chief of Production. His name was in the credits of many films and he met so many movie stars, writers, and politicians! I was very proud of him.)

Guy was not able to be present at the wedding. He wrote a poem, which he recorded. When the tape of his very touching poem was played at the ceremony, we all cried. There were not enough handkerchiefs for everyone. I knew I would miss him terribly, but life moves forward. I then moved to a new apartment with my husband and mother-in-law.

∞

Tunisia's Independence

I got married on December 25, 1962, in Tunis. Victor was working for the Customs Department, which was part of the government. He soon became the right hand of President Bourguiba. I found a job with the French Embassy in the pension section. After a few months, I became pregnant with our first child.

When there is a change in the political system, the opposition is sometimes encouraged to create disturbances. Hordes of young people took to the streets, burning Jewish stores, the synagogue, and some homes owned by the Jewish community. They surrounded the French Embassy, broke windows, and set fires around the bushes. Because of the unsafe situation, we packed a few suitcases in a hurry and booked the first flight we could get to Paris. We left behind everything we owned, but I was happy to get closer to Guy in France. He was already married and had a son.

It was a difficult adaptation. Parisians were in a bad mood and were showing their anger. They did not welcome so many refugees from Algeria, Tunisia, and Morocco. We found an apartment in a very popular district. I applied for a job with a company that used the first computers, which were operated with perforated cards. All the French banks were our customers.

Anne was born a few months after we arrived. Fifteen months later, Isabelle came into the world, then Nathalie, then Valerie — as I look back on it now, I wanted to recreate the family that I had lost. Life was peaceful but busy, with so many children so soon. My mother-in-law was very helpful, for which I owe her many thanks. In 1968, my husband received a job offer in New York. Again we packed whatever we had accumulated and flew to the United States.

We rented a house in Richmond Hill, Queens, across the street from a school. The neighbors were very kind; they helped us to get all of the necessary paperwork done so that we could become legal residents. The children learned English very quickly. The teachers welcomed the "Frenchies." I enrolled in a beauty school called the Wilfred Academy. I loved what I was learning, and after my graduation, pushed and encouraged by a wonderful, dedicated teacher, Mr. Lobbit, I opened a beauty salon in Great Neck in Nassau County.

Behind That Smile

The Salon

The new business was located forty-five minutes from my home. I met many wonderful people among my customers. Tamara Vassiliev and Phyllis Epstein became my best friends. Phyllis helped me to open a boutique in the salon and filled up the racks with colorful scarves and silk clothes. It was an innovative idea. Today many salons have boutiques to attract more business.

Tamara was teaching Russian at the time. She came every day to encourage me and to have some coffee. Every customer would challenge me because I was young. I enjoyed making them feel good about themselves by making them beautiful. We were not allowed to take care of gentlemen at that time; the rules were very strict. We would have needed a separate entrance and a separate room. I worked late hours and often on Sundays to prepare women for weddings and other special occasions.

In 1971, I became pregnant again. I worked until the last week before the due date. Our son, Charles, was born on May 31, Memorial Day! What a miracle after four lovely girls. When his sisters came to the hospital, they thought that the parade was to celebrate *bienvenue* to their new baby brother.

I was back at work after a week. I received such a warm welcome! My desk was covered with gifts and cards. It felt good to have been missed. At home, however, the atmosphere was cold. I did not realize that my husband had many affairs during those years. We eventually decided to divorce, but first we wanted to return to France. We sold our house and the business. After a garage sale, we packed only personal items. My mother-in-law had decided to move back in with her son once we arrived in Paris. Soon Victor, who had found a new companion, would disappear completely from our lives.

In France the social system helps large families to survive. We found an apartment in the suburbs of Paris, far from my brother, but he visited often. I found a job in a pharmaceutical company, part of Rhône-Poulenc. My oldest daughters, Anne and Isabelle, took care of the little ones until I got home at night. They were in school or kindergarten until 5:00 p.m.

Our First Vacation

After a year, the social services sent us for a vacation in the center of France. The country was breathtaking: forests, woods, and a long river called Le Lot where many small boats competed every weekend. The town was Cajarc. The man who would become President Pompidou was the mayor. We were directed to a little bungalow on the top of a hill. Every night after dinner, the social committee would organize a show or a craft demonstration. Saturday evenings were reserved for music and dancing. All the ladies were beautifully dressed and danced with their companions to the sound of the accordion.

I liked to sit in a corner with my children around me. I really looked like Mrs. Duck with my five ducklings. The second Saturday, as I was choosing my seat in a corner and calming down the children, a tall, handsome gentleman stood in front of me and invited me to dance. I became red like a poppy from embarrassment. He took my hand and I had no choice but to follow him. The kids were applauding as we were swirling among the dancers. Not one word was exchanged, other than a thank-you at the end of the dance. My heart was beating so hard, it was as if I had a drum inside my chest.

Most days we all walked to town to enjoy the outdoor market. The children were singing, running, and jumping, just happy to breathe fresh air and feel free. We filled up a few bags with fruit and vegetables and turned to walk toward our bungalow, singing and laughing. At the first turn of the hill, we saw four gentlemen sitting on a rock. Right away they came toward us, offering their help to carry the heavy bags.

My heart stopped right there. One of them was the handsome man I had danced with. His name was Jean-Luc. After a few questions, I learned he thought I must be a babysitter or one of the counselors. He was surprised to see me so young with such a large family. He offered to visit the town with us in his elegant car, a DS Citroën, which he had inherited from his father who had passed away a few months before. Our eyes met again, and Mr. Cupid sent his arrow.

Jean-Luc had been born in Algeria. He had to leave the country in 1962 when General de Gaulle agreed to give the native Algerians their independence. At seven years old, he moved to Paris with his father, a steward for Air France, a sister who was ten years old, and a handicapped mother, along with thousands of other French citizens. They had to relocate to a small apartment in the suburbs of Paris. It was a dramatic departure; they left behind all of their belongings and their Algerian friends and neighbors.

Jean-Luc went to elementary school, but it took him a long time to get used to his new life. After middle school, discouraged by some bad grades, his father decided to send him as an apprentice to a large hotel called Le Frantel. It was a fine, elegant building, located next to Orly Airport. Jean-Luc was sixteen then. His mentor and first chef was the famous Joël Robuchon, who today is well known for opening so many restaurants in Paris, New York, Las Vegas, Japan, and all over the world. He was thought of as the best chef during those years, and his cold and severe attitude scared his young helpers. The training was very difficult. There were strict rules to learn about classical French cooking. Jean-Luc became discouraged many times, but he forged ahead.

There were no young chefs at that time. Older cooks had to earn their promotions. Hierarchy was the rule. After a few years, Jean-Luc began to work for different companies in their cantines. He prepared and supervised other workers in order to feed thousands of employees. There were elaborate buffets with several choices. He learned speed, organization, and marketing, and he was successful in such positions. However, his dream was to open his own restaurant one day.

After three weeks of vacation, the children and I returned to Paris by train. Jean-Luc had driven us to the station. We exchanged addresses and telephone numbers. I went back to my job, certain that Jean-Luc would never reappear in my life.

I was wrong!

A week later, I received a telephone call at work. He had stayed a week longer in Cajarc and wanted to take me out during my lunchtime. My heart was hanging by a string! My colleague across from my desk saw how red my face was. She wanted to know why and asked so many questions!

Jean-Luc wanted to know everything about us. He realized how much we had missed during our years in New York, all of the good opportunities that had been abandoned because of the divorce. He was in love, and admitted that he had fallen in love with the children as well. Charles was three years old at the time and became very attached to Jean-Luc, who was ready to give up his family and his friends for us. Together we decided to attempt to return to this heaven called New York!

After many investigations and procedures by the U.S. Embassy, we received our green cards. Jean-Luc became my partner for life; he promised to help me raise my five children! What a wonderful man! We both handed in our resignations at work, sold our furniture, and prepared for our departure, the beginning of our great American adventure! We drove around to say goodbye to our families and friends, promising to come back soon. So many hugs, so many tears! We would be just one ocean away, but this was small consolation. Jean-Luc was frustrated because he did not speak any English. He was regretting not having taken his classes more seriously. The children consoled him. They would be his teachers!

∽

Behind That Smile

New York, New York

I f I can make it there, I'll make it anywhere," sang
Frank Sinatra.

We will try!

We arrived at JFK Airport on October 31, 1977. It
was Halloween. We filled the yellow cab with our luggage.
We had so much that the trunk could not close properly.
During the ride, we bounced from deep pothole to deep
pothole, each of which encouraged a curse from the driver. In the streets, the children were disguised. As part of
their Halloween rituals, they were throwing eggs all over
the car and the windshield. Jean-Luc was surprised and
soon grew angry: "How do they know we are French?" he
asked. We laughed and explained the tradition. It was not
directed at him personally.

The taxi entered Ozone Park, where our Italian
friends — Marie and Signor Tony Sorace, whom I knew
from my first trip to America — gave us hospitality. They
were a family of eight, but they opened their hearts, their
door, and their kitchen. They refused any financial help
until we could find an apartment. We drove around, and
after two weeks we found a place in Great Neck, above

a coffee shop, two blocks from my former beauty shop. The owners, Nick and Agnes, were so happy to meet Jean-Luc and to see the children so grown up. It was wonderful!

I don't have enough words to describe their generosity and their kindness.

Nick had come from Greece. He remembered how difficult it was to start a new life in America. Agnes had come from Scotland. They had four young children. Most days all of us met in the park at sundown to chat. Jean-Luc was learning English very quickly and so he enjoyed participating in the conversations. During the day, he would help in the kitchen. Nick taught me how to take orders from customers and, when necessary, how to handle the difficult ones. He knew that our dream was to have a restaurant of our own one day.

Jean-Luc would go on interviews for positions as chef or kitchen helper, but it was impossible for him to find a position without the necessary language. After many attempts, we both applied for jobs at the Brasserie St. Germain, a fine, elegant French restaurant located on the Miracle Mile in Manhasset. What beautiful décor! The different sections of the restaurant were large; all of the seats were very comfortable. The owners had brought the idea for wood-oven pizza to the United States from the South of France. I learned how to be a waitress, and my boss, Mr. Bruno, gave me wonderful advice. His wife, Lucette (the "blonde one"), was very friendly and taught me how to organize the seating arrangements and the reception area.

On Sundays the restaurant organized a huge buffet — cold salads, croissants, hot dishes, pastries — it was 1977, and this was one of the first such buffets in an American restaurant. Mr. Bruno and his associates also owned The Patisserie and La Crêpe, both of which were also located on the Miracle Mile. I tried everything that was offered for dessert so that I could better advise the patrons about their choices. Jean-Luc was hired as a chef for the dinner shift. He learned more English and some Spanish, and he could speak French on a regular basis. A perfect combination! We both worked long hours. We took care of the children by taking turns with our work schedules. It was difficult at times, but we always kept in mind our dream to one day open our own little place!

Mark Twain said, "The secret of getting ahead is getting started."

We were officially started in America.

Charles (center) at his bar mitzvah with our great friends
Jeanne and Emile Tubiana

What a Small World

The children started school at Great Neck North. After a week, they arrived home all excited. They had met a girl named Viviane who spoke French and whose father had been born in Tunisia, in my home town of Béja. A few days later, we kissed and hugged Emile and Jeanne Tubiana as if we had always known them. They were two more angels who helped to guide us on our path. Emile knew the parents I had lost! He was touched by our hard work and by the courage it took to move our family to New York. He promised to help us along on our ambitious journey.

Lucette outside La Baraka

II

La Baraka

Behind That Smile

Eureka!

It was a Wednesday in April 1979. Jean-Luc and I had just come home from work. It had been a busy night at Brasserie St. Germain. As we entered, the telephone was ringing. It was Emile Tubiana. "Could you meet me in Little Neck? There is an empty store I would like to show you." It was already 10:00 p.m. The kids had done their homework and were watching a movie. We rushed to the address on Northern Boulevard. The place was large enough for a decent-sized restaurant. It needed a lot of repairs, of course, as well as all of the permits to do the work. We were excited, but at the same time scared by this heavy responsibility.

Emile and Jeanne offered their financial help right away. They refused, to this day, to be reimbursed. So many angels opened the doors to our dreams! Our hearts are still filled with love and gratitude. Unfortunately, many of our wonderful friends are now gone. We wish that they could have enjoyed our successful enterprise with us.

La Baraka was born! We took the name from a very romantic song written by the great Charles Aznavour. It means "blessings, good luck, and prayers" – all would be needed for us to accomplish our wishes and our dreams.

Behind That Smile

Queens on Wheels

The painters, the carpenters, and the plumbers went to work. The banging and knocking went on every evening until dawn. We had two months to accomplish all of the work — the opening date was set for July 14, 1979, to celebrate Bastille Day, the Fourth of July of France.

One morning Jean-Luc received some bad news. His mother had to be hospitalized. He took an overnight plane to France to be by her side. After he left, I was in charge of getting all of the permits from the building department. The day I had planned to do the paperwork, I got up very early to beat the traffic and be at the office when they opened. I was driving a huge van that we had purchased a few months after our arrival in the United States. It had large, custom windows and huge wheels. The van was convenient in that it could carry the whole family and still have room for the supplies that we needed for the restaurant. I parked the van on Queens Boulevard, put all of the necessary quarters in the parking meter, and proceeded to the building. I had to find the specific office where one could get the permits.

An angel was sitting at the desk, a middle-aged man with a friendly smile. He welcomed me and helped me to fill out all of the forms and questionnaires. He then wished me "Good luck!" and promised to come to the restaurant for dinner with his family. I completed my tasks and came down to the lobby with a light heart, blessing Mr. Perlmutter for making the process so easy. As I walked to the meter, I promised myself that I would enjoy the rest of the beautiful, sunny morning.

The spot was empty! My head started to spin! I knew that I had parked the car right there, right here! Where was it? A tow truck passed next to me. I asked the driver if he had taken my van. I still had time on the meter. I was horrified by his answer.

"No, ma'am! A car is stolen here every five minutes. You are across the street from the courthouse and the prisoners. They often try to escape!" I didn't know what to do. "Oh my God! Help me," I prayed. I had so much to do, and I was so far away from the restaurant. I went back to my angel in the building. Within five minutes, I was surrounded by five employees, including Mr. Perlmutter, who offered to call 911 for me. I was sobbing. What was I going to say to Jean-Luc, whose return was scheduled in two days? After the police report was completed, one of the inspectors offered to drive me back to Little Neck. It turned out that his house was two blocks away from La Baraka.

The van was found the next day, a few blocks away from where it had disappeared. It had been completely stripped, from the large wheels to the windows to the seats. All of the stolen equipment was eventually found in a garage in Jamaica, in a place called Nice People Garage. The police investigated and took away all of the criminals involved. The insurance helped us by providing a loaner car, repairing all of the damage, and replacing what was lost.

Behind That Smile

The Opening

The days went by so fast. We were very close to the July 14, 1979, opening date. The restaurant slowly began to take shape. The tables were set with white and brown tablecloths, the chairs were in place, and the kitchen equipment was in working condition. We were ready to go! Jean-Luc began to think about where to shop for fresh vegetables and other delicacies. We sat long hours trying to decide on a menu and on our prices.

All of the children helped. Everyone had a duty and a responsibility. The restaurant looked like a hive, and all the bees were busy. Charles, our son, who was six years old at the time, was in charge of cleaning the string beans. To complete his task more quickly, half of the string beans went into the garbage pail. We had to buy another bag in order to fill up the pan.

We established a list of guests for the opening reception on July 13. We were so excited, so nervous, and so anxious, all at the same time. Jean-Luc's wish to open his own restaurant was about to come true!

BEHIND THAT SMILE

The Reception on July 13

The day finally came. We had to prepare some appetizers at home because the ovens were full of chickens and ducks. The girls decorated the trays for the cold appetizers and set up a long buffet under Isabelle's supervision.

We arrived a little after our guests, in a van filled with hot food. We had four trays full of *bestel* — strudel filled with meat or spinach or cheese — it smelled so good in the car! We parked in the back of the restaurant. When Jean-Luc opened the doors, Charles wanted to be the first one to go out. In his excitement, he stepped on all of the trays, smashing half of them! I saw lightning coming out of Jean-Luc's eyes, which was followed by an assortment of curses in French. We managed to save some of those delicacies. In the end, there was plenty of food. The guests enjoyed everything on the buffet. We did not see Charles the whole night. He must have been hiding under a table! Everyone congratulated us for our good work and for the courage it took to realize our dream.

First Lunch

We decided to open for lunch on weekdays and every evening for dinner. The first lunch was on a Monday; two people, a lady and a gentleman, pushed through the door at 11:30. They must have come from one of the offices in the neighborhood. They clearly had a limited time for their meal.

They ordered an omelet and a hamburger. The kitchen was delayed in making the preparations because of the lateness of incoming deliveries. I requested many times to pick up their order. It seemed that suddenly all of our clocks were running too fast! The two guests started to show their impatience, and I too became impatient. Jean-Luc had just finished seasoning the chopped meat and was forming a ball with it. I entered the kitchen again, growling about the delay. The chef became angry and, like a bolt of lightning, a red ball of meat landed on my hair. Any baseball pitcher would have been proud! This was followed by an exclamation, the tone of which you can imagine: "Out of my kitchen!"

I pushed open the door to the dining room, red like a cooked lobster from embarrassment, not to mention the red meat in my hair from what had been the hamburger. I apologized to the couple: "Your meal will be out in a few minutes!" The gentleman looked at me with an amused expression. "That's OK," he said. "It is late for us. We have to get back to work." They left a tip on the table and off they went. We never saw them again. What a shame!

Big Heart

When we first opened, we had just some letters on the top of the wall outside the restaurant – La Baraka. It was plain, and perhaps too discreet for some people to find. We learned later that many people passed the restaurant because they could not see the sign. One of our regular patrons suggested that we should install an awning to enhance the business. Unfortunately, we could not take on such an expense at that time. Perhaps later we would think about an awning.

Mr. and Mrs. Rubin, who made the suggestion, must have investigated the price of such an addition to our restaurant. The following week they came for dinner. After coffee and dessert, they asked us to sit down. They had prepared an envelope with a check for five thousand dollars! The surprise, and the tears that followed, kept us speechless. What a generous gift! We promised to reimburse them – slowly – but they refused. We soon installed a beautiful, elegant awning.

Thank you, Mr. and Mrs. Rubin, for your help, for filling the restaurant with your family and friends, and for celebrating so many birthdays and anniversaries with us. Mr. Rubin told us that when he started his own business, he had been helped by friends, and he had promised himself that he would be of help to others in the future. We miss you, and your jokes, very much!

∞

Behind That Smile

Home Sweet Home

One day, as I was shopping at the supermarket, I met one of the patrons from the beauty shop. She was so happy to see me! After many questions, she took my number and promised to call me.

We met the next day. It turned out that her father was selling his house in a little alley in Great Neck across from the junior high school. Knowing that we did not have money or credit yet, she offered to give us the mortgage with no down payment. We fell in love with that little cottage, surrounded by trees and bushes. What an opportunity! We visited the house many times. Finally, we left the apartment above the coffee shop, thanking Nick and Agnes a thousand times. We were moving only a few blocks away, and so we promised to meet in the park again. We so enjoyed painting and decorating that little cottage. It was a piece of jewelry in our eyes. Thank you, Mrs. Ginsberg, for helping us to fulfill our American dream.

Behind That Smile

Another Dream

Jean-Luc is a motorcycle rider. When he was sixteen years old, his parents offered him a motorcycle for his birthday. When we lived in Paris, we attended every reunion of motorcycle enthusiasts around the Place de la Bastille. Hundreds of young people would get together. The night would eventually end at a restaurant near Les Halles, the famous food market.

After we had decided to immigrate to New York, Jean-Luc sold his motorcycle to finance part of the trip. When we arrived in 1977, he would always notice when a Corvette passed us on the highway. That iconic car became part of his American dream. However, it was impossible for him to rent or buy one at that time. "How come so many people are driving them?" he would ask. I had to point out to him that "Those drivers are of a certain age, with gray hair or no hair. They probably had to work very hard for a long time to afford such a car."

Twenty years later, Jean-Luc took me by the hand one day. He showed me a beautiful, elegant yellow Corvette in a dealership window. He also showed me the top of his head. Only a little hair was left! "Now is the time!" he said. "I waited patiently and worked very hard!"

"Patience is the art of hope," said Luc de Clapiers, marquis de Vauvenargues, the eighteenth-century French moralist and philosopher. Jean-Luc's patience had finally paid off!

∽

Nathalie, Isabelle, Charles, and Valerie, 1984

Anne, 1984

Newspaper Critics

Two weeks after the opening, there were people at a large table who ordered many different main courses. I had a feeling that one of them must have been a restaurant critic. The Sunday following that dinner, we received a lot of telephone calls from our friends. We were listed in *The New York Times* with a few stars. The Tunisian couscous, which we really introduced into New York, made the headline. The days following that glowing article, La Baraka filled up with curious, hungry people. Some older couples congratulated us because the couscous reminded them of the cuisine in North Africa when they were stationed there as part of the Allied forces during World War II. *The Daily News* and *Newsday* also sent anonymous critics. Their reviews drew further large crowds to our small restaurant.

Those days inspired the title of the third section of my story, "Pressure Cooker." We were "boiling" with energy and ambition, and La Baraka was "steaming" with people. Valerie stayed by our side to help when her schedule permitted it. The other children eventually moved to other states, following their companions or husbands-to-be.

Jean-Luc and Lucette visiting Tunisia in 1984

III

Pressure Cooker

❧

I've collected some stories — some funny, some awkward, some poignant — from our years at La Baraka. Every time we open the door at the restaurant, it is a blessing. We have at times had to face some difficult situations and strange requests, but we have always done our best. Our goal is to avoid the French words that are sometimes heard at establishments in Manhattan:

"C'est impossible!"

Behind That Smile

The Madam

An elderly couple entered the restaurant one night for dinner. I asked the lady in front of me, "What is the name on the reservation, madame?" When she told me, I asked them to follow me to their table. As we walked, I heard the gentleman arguing with her: "I told you when you came out of the house that you looked like a madam. Even the waitress noticed it!" I felt terrible when I heard his remark. I must admit that she must have applied her makeup in a dark place.

Her lips looked like a heartbeat from the electrocardiogram machine, and her eyebrows reminded me of Groucho Marx. I sat her at a table, but her husband had already seated himself at another table far away from her. It cost me a lot of patience and a lot of patting on the back and soothing words to convince him to sit with his companion. He finally got up, went over, and apologized to her, wiping her wet eyes, which spread the *rimmel* all over. He gave her a kiss on the lips, which replicated the heartbeat on his mouth. I only smiled — somehow I managed to keep from bursting into laughter at this funny scene. They had a glass of wine, talked like teenagers, and enjoyed their meals. As they were leaving, smiling and holding hands, the patrons at the tables close to them, who had noticed the dilemma, applauded. It was like a wedding reception! What a relief for us that things turned out as they did.

Behind That Smile

Perfume Vendor

As Christmastime approaches, we see a lot of vendors at the door: toys, clothes, and perfumes, especially imitation perfumes. One afternoon in December, one young man after another showed up and tried to sell us their merchandise. Very politely I declined their offers. After a few of these solicitors, I perhaps became less pleasant. After a cold "No, thank you!" to the latest salesman, I turned my back and went toward the kitchen. The gentleman followed me a few steps and called me: "Miss, miss!" He then showed me his badge. Oh God! He was a health department inspector! His badge very closely resembled the vendors' badges!

All restaurants dread their visits. He conducted his inspection thoroughly, in a terrible mood. He gave us a few violations just to show his authority and his power. From that day on, I have not lost my patience and have given a big smile to every vendor at the door — especially those with a badge!

Behind That Smile

In God We Trust,

Not Always in Others

Through the years, we have had many dedicated waiters and busboys. Some became part of the family. We had workers from many different nationalities and traditions: Russian, Malaysian (the wonderful James), Romanian (the beautiful Monica; Ran and his brother Andre; and our adopted daughter Gabriella, who prepared all of the menus, the special occasion cards, and the holiday invitations).

At one time, we hired three young boys from the neighborhood. They did not take their jobs seriously, but because we knew their parents, we had to keep them on the job. One night, one of the mothers came for dinner with a friend. As soon as she entered the restaurant, she hugged me powerfully and kissed me all over my face. "Thank you! Thank you for all of the mussels, all of the lamb chops, and the bottles of Châteauneuf-du-Pape that you sent to us via our son!" These were items that had been missing on a regular basis. We had tried to catch the thieves for a while. Now we knew where these items went. Of course we found an excuse and let him go. His friends soon followed.

Here is a story written by Voltaire, the famous philosopher who lived during the reign of Louis XIV:

In the past, one of the kings of France was looking for an honest man to become the Minister of Finance. His men had posted written notices on the trees. Many people lined up in front of the castle gate. In order to meet the king in his office, the candidates had to come through a corridor where bags of gold coins were lined up.

When the first man presented himself, the king ordered him to jump and dance. His pockets were so filled with stolen coins that he could not budge. He was put in jail immediately. The second and third candidates met similar fates. The fourth person who came through the door danced so lightly and elegantly that he became the Minister of Finance that the king was looking for. Honesty always pays!

At least our former employees stayed out of jail!

Orah nursing Robinson, the cat

Our Faithful Companion

When we came from France in 1977, we had to leave behind our beautiful German shepherd named Orah. She was as pretty – and as big – as the famous Rin Tin Tin. It was my brother's responsibility to send us the dog as soon as we had settled down. After a year had passed, we contacted Guy. He then called to let us know that Orah would be arriving by plane later that week.

After many administrative formalities and our providing proof that Orah had all of the required vaccines, we opened the cage. She jumped so high when she saw us! Both we and the dog were crying with joy. It took a while before we all calmed down.

We kept Orah's arrival from the children. It would be a surprise. After school, as they walked home, Orah saw them from far away, carrying their school bags. When we let her loose, the children jumped as high as Orah. The reunion was very touching. With their eyes filled with tears, they could not thank us enough for the return of their beloved friend. For the first week, we took the dog to the backyard of the restaurant. We did not want her to feel lonely in a new place. We also knew that she did not like bad weather, especially thunder.

One very busy night at the restaurant, as rain drops began to come down, we went to catch Orah to give her shelter. She was not there! This was a mystery, as the gate was closed.

Where had she gone?

The room quickly filled up with hungry patrons. We were worried about her, but we had to get back to work. After a few minutes, a lady called me: "Miss! Miss! There is a bag under my table. It's not mine. Maybe someone else forgot it." I lifted the tablecloth. There was Orah, shivering. She was scared, and so was the lady! It took all of Jean-Luc's strength to pull her out from under the table and get her down to the basement. As nervous as she was, we thanked God that she did not bite the lady. We were also lucky that a health inspector was not in the restaurant. It is a no-no — which can lead to a big fine and even to the closing of a restaurant — to have an animal in the proximity of the food.

Orah remained a wonderful friend to our family for many years. We still think of her fondly today.

Guy, Jean-Luc, and Lucette, first anniversary, 1980

Do Not Judge a Book
by Its Cover

It was a Wednesday, which is often a slow day in the restaurant. At 5:00 p.m., a gentleman came to the door. He said that he was waiting for his fiancée and chose a table in front. He sat down and removed his hat. His hair stood on end like a cornfield. When he removed his jacket, his T-shirt had more holes than Swiss cheese. He did not smell like a rose, and he soon began scratching himself. I gave him a menu; he held it upside down but was apparently still trying to read it. I panicked. I realized that I was in trouble, so I called Jean-Luc to my rescue. The stranger was claiming very loudly that "Jesus Christ had sent him!" Very politely, Jean-Luc asked him to put his hat and coat back on and to wait for the lady outside, in exchange for two large sandwiches. The lady never came, and we had to disinfect the whole area before any other customers arrived. Oops!

Behind That Smile

The Devil Made

Me Do It

It was a Tuesday night. There were not too many reservations on the book. A couple of friends called us to join them for coffee and dessert. It was a pleasure to go out and relax. About two hours later, we drove in front of the restaurant, which was closed by then. Next to the door, under the tree, our dishwasher was standing, a bottle of wine in his mouth, held straight out like a trumpet! We were shocked to see this, but we were in the middle lane so we could not stop our car. We turned around as quickly as we could and returned to La Baraka. The "musician" was gone, leaving his bottle on the grass.

The next morning, we were waiting for the guilty party, his bottle in our hands. "Did you take this bottle last night?" Jean-Luc asked. The employee became pale and tears started to pour out of his eyes. "It wasn't me! The devil made me do it!" He apologized many times and promised to behave in the future, begging us to not fire him. After some consultation, we gave him a reprieve.

Behind That Smile

A Man from Mars

One night, around 8:00 p.m., we had almost every table filled with customers. We were all busy taking care of their requests. I noticed a gentleman at the door. He was well groomed, wearing an elegant suit and tie. Before I could ask if he had a reservation, he rushed toward a couple sitting at a back table. I thought, "He must know them."

On the contrary, they were surprised by his presence. He asked for the time ... 8:00 p.m. ... and the year ... 1985. He panicked at their answer: "I'm too late for my job!" He turned around and ran outside, pushing aside a couple who had just come in. Who was he? We apologized to the lady and gentleman at the back table, who were still stunned by what had happened. We never found out who he was, and we never saw him again. You never know who will push in the door. So many planets surround us!

BEHIND THAT SMILE

Wong and

the Wrong Family

It was a Saturday night at 7:30 p.m. The restaurant was very crowded. A reservation had been made under "Wong Family for Six People." When they arrived, five of the party sat down. They were waiting for the father, who was parking the car. After a few minutes had gone by, an older gentleman entered. I thought he was Mr. Wong and took him to the Wongs' table. He sat down and picked up a menu. As he was reading it, he didn't realize that everybody was looking at him, wondering who he was. He was certainly not the man they were waiting for. When he finally looked around, he panicked, jumped out of his chair, and apologized profusely to the party. Not only was it not his family, but he was not even in the right restaurant!

He took a breath, returned to the table, and politely bowed to the Wongs, who were laughing at his mistake. Everyone took it in the right spirit.

"Tradition, Tradition!"

BEHIND THAT SMILE

Out of My Kitchen—Again!

O ut of my kitchen!" shouted the chef, my husband, as I was waiting with visible impatience to pick up an order. I was only being myself, a Taurus according to the zodiac. As I waited, I started to straighten the spice bottles that were located above me on the shelf. By accident, a big tin box of bay leaves fell on the other side, on the chef's head! Before it touched the floor, he kicked it so hard (thanks to his training in soccer!) that the violence of the strike opened the door to the dining room. A cloud of bay leaves followed me from the kitchen like a green veil behind a bride. "Out of my kitchen!" he repeated. All of the heads turned to look at me.

I had to pass in front of all of the tables, red as a beet, with half a smile on my face to hide my embarrassment. I stayed in the coatroom until the last customer had left the restaurant. Jean-Luc came to get me out of my hiding place with a bunch of parsley, as it was too late to get me flowers. A word to the wise — never make a French chef angry during a rush-hour service — or any other time!

Mmm! How Good

Is This Chocolate Cake!

One Saturday night, the dining room was full of customers. We always called it "Saturday night fever." On this evening, almost everyone came at the same time. One could easily have had a panic attack, but we know that we cannot show our anxiety. We tried to satisfy all of the patrons with a smile.

At about 8:00 p.m., an older gentleman sitting at a table for six became very pale and eventually fainted. His family panicked; his son laid him on the floor and we called 911. His table, of course, was located close to the kitchen, so he was blocking the "traffic," which made it difficult to serve the other customers. The plates were getting cold, and the meats were probably getting more cooked than was required. The party of six had finished their meal; their desserts were already on the table. Ten minutes went by, which seemed like hours in this situation. Some volunteers were now around the gentleman, tapping on his cheeks and talking to him, which further blocked the flow.

After the first moments of fear and emotion, while we were still waiting for the ambulance to arrive, his wife sat back down at the table. She slowly ate all of her chocolate cake, and she finished her husband's cake as well! She was now calm in the midst of a tumultuous Saturday night. When the family left with the paramedics, every table ordered chocolate cake for dessert. It had to be good, since the concerned lady ate two portions! We did not have enough cake to satisfy everyone, so a few patrons had to leave without tasting that wonderful cake.

Behind That Smile

Little Neck Falls

It was a Wednesday afternoon in September 1983. We had finished serving lunch to our customers and had begun to clean the salad bar plates and chafing dishes. The last diners were two ladies, Marion and Diane. They were having an enjoyable conversation and asked permission to stay a little longer as they hadn't seen each other for quite a few years. It was a cloudy day. The sky to the west was gray and the horizon was dark; this usually meant that a storm was on its way. Soon a few drops of rain began to fall, followed by showers with thunder and lightning.

Northern Boulevard, especially our block, gets flooded often because the sewer system cannot evacuate heavy rain quickly enough. Within thirty minutes, the street became a river. Cars and buses splashed great sprays of water to the level of the stores. The torrential rain continued. Soon the water came up to the doorknob. We could see only the tops of the parking meters. The two ladies and our staff became very concerned about this dangerous situation.

The ladies' car was soon spotted, floating like a boat in the middle of the boulevard-turned-river. Some kids from the neighborhood got out their surfboards and enjoyed the ride, swerving to avoid the vehicles. What a picturesque and unusual sight! Marion and Diane started to cry when they saw their car floating in the middle of the block. We wanted to help, but we could not open the door. There was nothing to do but watch and wait.

In the meantime, the telephone kept ringing. People were asking for reservations for dinner. Where could they have been calling from? Did they not have this same weather? Finally, after an hour, the rain stopped and the sewer system began to catch up. As the water was sucked off the street, the sidewalk began to clear. We could finally open the door. The carpet was soaked all the way to the kitchen. Marion and Diane called their husbands for help, and they finally went on their way. It was 4:00 p.m. We vacuumed the water and excess moisture as best we could, hoping that by 5:00 or 6:00, we would be able to accommodate all of the reservations.

What a coincidence! We sold so many fish dishes that night! During service, one lady called me over to her table. "Miss, miss, I think the carpet is a little wet under my feet!" If she only knew what we had gone through that afternoon. She must have just come off a flight from the Bahamas!

∾

Blind Date

One night, at dinnertime, a lady came in alone and chose a corner table. She was of middle age and very elegant. She was waiting for a date — a blind date — whose name was Mr. Maurice. A few reservations arrived; I was busy seating the patrons and taking a few requests. I also sat a beautiful blonde lady in another corner of the room. She was waiting for her husband. They would be celebrating their second wedding anniversary.

I noticed a gentleman standing next to my desk, trying to get my attention. He gave me his name and asked me to point discreetly to Mrs. Doris. He was French. He was also very elegant, with a black suit and a red tie. When I pointed to the left, he nodded with a grimace and rushed to the right corner where he discovered the attractive blonde woman. He sat and ordered two glasses of wine without talking to her. What a rude personage!

The blonde lady panicked. What if her husband had arrived at that moment? I apologized to her and explained that the gentleman had made a mistake. The man, however, did not budge. Thank goodness our

conversation was in French so very few of our customers could understand my angry words. He finally left,
throwing his napkin to the floor. In the meantime, Mrs.
Doris was waiting, patiently sipping a drink. I told her
that Mr. Maurice had called and was unable to make it
tonight. Did she want to stay for dinner? She was sad but
ordered a meal, looking constantly at her phone. I hope
that she will have more luck in the future.

The blonde woman's husband arrived soon after-
ward. A very close call! I don't think she mentioned her
other "date."

Face-Lift

We originally rented the restaurant space from a very nice, very tolerant landlord. When he passed away, we had been running La Baraka for eight years. As we did not have a signed lease, we thought it would be best if we could figure out a way to buy the building. It was, and still is, a very old building for the area. After running from one bank to another, we took the big step. It was a wonderful feeling to know that we were the landlords. We also realized that we were now responsible for any and all repairs that had to be made. The kitchen needed to be renovated before anything else.

The contractor needed five days minimum to do the job. We had to close the restaurant during all of that time. I thought to put a sign in the window that would be a little less stressful than "Closed for Renovation" because many people would read it as "Out of Business." So I wrote, "Closed for a Face-Lift." The job was finished by Friday morning, so we could prepare everything for the weekend as usual.

At the opening for dinner that night, customers rushed in, happy to see us and to see the restaurant freshly painted. Many of them shared their anxiety that we would never reopen. As I was taking an order at a table, I noticed a lady adjusting her glasses and looking at my face very closely. She said aloud to her companion, "They did not do a bad job. Maybe I should get the name and address?" She clearly believed that I had gotten the face-lift!

Would I advertise in the window if I was going for a face-lift?

∽

BEHIND THAT SMILE

New Year's Eve Celebration

The 2015 New Year's Celebration was very special. So many years had gone by like lightning. The dining room was decorated with lights and garlands. Jean-Luc prepared a succulent menu with several wonderful choices. The whole staff was dressed up with red ties and suits. We had two seatings; the second started at 9:00 p.m. We had hired a musician, a "one-woman band." She played guitar, bazooka, and harmonica; she knew popular songs from different countries; and she also kept the crowd laughing with her jokes. We had also hired a belly dancer; she arrived at 10:30, all dressed up in a red and gold outfit. She began to perform among the tables to Mediterranean music.

Suddenly a woman called me to her table. Her husband was not feeling well. He was as pale as the wall. We brought ice to place on his neck and forehead, but the lady insisted that we call 911. In the meantime, the belly dancer had climbed on a chair to let all of the guests appreciate her talents. As she was dancing, six firemen and nurses entered through the front door. It was very stressful for us, but the diners may have thought that it was part of the act. A nurse took the gentleman's pulse, while a few of the firemen were looking at the beautiful dancer, who was still on a chair. Her time was limited to forty minutes because she had another job at a far-away venue. So she kept right on dancing. The sick man eventually began to feel better. He answered a few questions from the medical staff, who wanted him to go to the hospital as a precaution. He refused to go, however, choosing instead to finish his dinner and see what was going to happen next.

As the first responders were packing up, the singer went back on. The firemen walked with "snail steps" to the door because they wanted to see the rest of the show. After they left, everyone got up to dance, even though the space was limited. The belly dancer took the formerly sick man by the hand and made him dance. When the time came, we all counted the twelve strikes of the clock for midnight. We hugged one another and wished a "Happy New Year" to all.

Thank you to all of the people who made the night so special: the singer, the belly dancer, the firemen, the nurses, and, of course, our customers. Special thanks go to the wine and champagne!

Valerie, Gabriella, Lucette, and Michaela at
Mardi Gras, 2006

Popeye Double

Wednesday night is usually the slowest night of the week. We often organize a "theme night" — Bouillabaisse Night or New Orleans Night or Mediterranean Night, to name a few. Not only does the menu follow the theme, but we also provide the appropriate music. We chose Bouillabaisse Night for Wednesday, November 4, 2015. The accordionist whom we had called was not available. We needed one *tout de suite*.

The week before, Jean-Luc and I had decided to escape to a restaurant in Astoria for a romantic dinner. Astoria is a lively, colorful neighborhood; a lot of young people, many of them Greek, were sitting at outdoor *cafés* and walking from place to place. We parked our car and strolled up Ditmars Boulevard looking for a place to eat. We passed in front of a gentleman who was leaning against a wall, playing the smallest accordion I had ever seen. A cap covered his head, he wore a striped T-shirt, and with the pipe in his mouth he was the picture of Popeye. The only things missing were the muscled arms and a can of spinach. We stood there, at first dumbfounded and then entertained. Jean-Luc and I looked at each other and in a split second we had the same idea: "How about if we hire him for the bouillabaisse event?" We listened to his music for a while and eventually we struck up a conversation. His name was Carl. He lived in New Jersey and had traveled to Astoria by subway. We exchanged our names and telephone numbers, and eventually arranged for him to come and play for us. We gave him a little deposit and expected him to be in Little Neck on November 4 at 6:00 p.m. On the way home, we talked about his resemblance to Popeye, which was quite startling.

The week went by. We were so busy preparing for this special night that we didn't give our musician a second thought. Making bouillabaisse is a bit complicated. It's a fish soup made from the bones and heads. After draining the bones, we have a stock. We then cook sliced fish, mussels, clams, and a lobster, with a tomato base and some saffron flavoring. It is served with a cup of rouille, which is mashed potatoes with garlic and saffron, to be spread on the croutons. The room was decorated with hanging cardboard seafood. Every waiter was dressed as a sailor, with a striped shirt and a cap.

It was 6:30. The guests were starting to arrive. I became concerned about Carl. He was already late. I wondered if he was going to keep his promise to us. I constantly looked toward the door. Suddenly the sound of music came from outside. It was him —

"Popeye"! He was playing a few doors away. A crowd had surrounded him. It turned out that he had misunderstood us. We needed him inside the restaurant! After collecting a few tips from the crowd, he pushed open the door, still playing. What a surprise for the diners! Everyone wanted to know where we had found him. He was very funny, sometimes making exaggerated "Popeye" faces to make the people laugh. Besides the delicious bouillabaisse, he was the highlight of the evening. Bravo, Popeye!

The Banana Duck

L a Baraka had become very well known for our roasted duck. Jean-Luc buys a large amount of poultry. Every day he cooks a full tray, well done, in order to remove the fat from under the duck skin. I will not give you the recipe because your kitchen would then be on fire from the grease and full of smoke. When he is finished, each duck is delicious and succulent. We serve it with a choice of three sauces: orange, peach, or raspberry. We never have enough duck on weekends to satisfy the connoisseurs.

For many weeks, one of our regular customers would ask if the chef would make him a banana sauce. Every week I would put in my request and every week I would get the same angry answer from the chef: "We have so many choices of sauce. Why doesn't he try them all?" One week this customer made a reservation for four people at 7:30 p.m. He walked through the door dragging behind him a gigantic bunch of bananas! In an arrogant tone, he said, "Now ask the chef to make a banana sauce for me!" What an embarrassment! How could I push open the kitchen door and make that request again? After I began, Jean-Luc started yelling. He soon went out the back door and into the street. He was so angry that he had left his jacket by the door. After he had made his way around to the front, he was still yelling. Every head turned toward the famous front door. I stood there, completely frozen, holding the bananas.

Finally I shook myself off, took out a pan, and improvised a banana sauce with some cognac. I was not too proud of the sauce, or of myself, as I am not a great cook, but a customer had made a request and I felt I had no choice but to grant it. I then served the crispy duck, covered with banana sauce. The gentleman was very pleased. He came back regularly to La Baraka, but he never again asked for banana sauce. It must have been my cooking! I tried my best, and in the end I was happy. I had not lost a regular customer, nor had I lost my chef and husband!

Behind That Smile

Beheaded Fish

One of our specialties each week is a filet of sole with garlic, mushrooms, and herbs encased in dough in the shape of a fish. We finish it on the top with two eyes made out of black peppercorns and a piece of dough in the shape of a gill. When the fish is baked, the dough rises; it arrives at the table as delicious as it looks. It is a very popular dish. Most of our patrons love it.

One Saturday night, the dining room was full. We looked like little ants, scurrying from table to table to ensure that everyone was satisfied with their choices. One of our female customers had ordered the *sole en croûte*. As I brought it to her table, I was struck by how beautiful the sculpted fish looked. When the fish was put in front of the lady, however, she screamed and almost fell off her chair. Everyone looked at her; Jean-Luc came running from the kitchen to help. We were all very concerned until she said, "I don't want to see the head! Take it away from me!" After a moment, some of us began to laugh. She could not understand that it was all dough and not a real fish head. Jean-Luc, however, was not laughing. He was furious! He took the plate away, chopped the "head" off that poor filet of sole, and brought the dish back himself. "Here! No more head!"

He then stormed back into the kitchen. After half an hour, the lady called me over to her table. She apologized for having acted like a fool and, most importantly, asked that I report to the chef that her fish was delicious.

∽

Behind That Smile

Coda

As I finished writing the stories that make up "Pressure Cooker," I considered that our thirty-eight years at La Baraka have gone by so fast! We've had so many happy moments and shared so many important celebrations with our friends. We've also had our share of hardships and difficulties, but if one can smile and look beyond one's immediate troubles to the "big picture," it is possible to put even the most trying events into perspective. We will never forget all of the wonderful, generous, and friendly people whom we have met, those who believed in us and gave us the strength and courage to go on. To borrow a saying from Jewish wisdom:

"Who gives should never remember;
Who receives should never forget."

We will never forget!

Finally, all of my love and gratitude go to Jean-Luc, who trusted me to fulfill his dream, which became our dream. When I look back at my past, from the rubble of a bombed-out building to our successes at La Baraka seven decades later, the ambition, the resilience, and the tenacity that grew out of my childhood years have helped me to overcome all of the obstacles and pitfalls that destiny has placed in my way. I have learned how precious life is, and how the best way to live is one day at a time. At the worst moments of my life, I have always remembered that the sun will rise tomorrow, and that what seem like problems today will become the stories that we will laugh about in the future.

To my five children, Anne, Isabelle, Nathalie, Valerie, and Charles, to my twelve grandchildren, and to my six great-grandchildren:

May you have the drive and the energy to fulfill your wishes and your dreams! Keep your chin up, follow the star that twinkles above your head, and *la baraka* will be with you always.

To all of my family and friends – To Life!

Guy and Lucette

CPSIA information can be obtained
at www.ICGtesting.com
Printed in the USA
BVOW10*0437301117
501335BV00011B/159/P